0508729

Migration

Monica Hughes

Heinemann Library
Chicago, Illinois

Editorial: Jilly Attwood, Kate Bellamy
Design: Jo Hinton-Malivoire
Picture research: Ginny Stroud-Lewis, Ruth Blair
Production: Séverine Ribierre

Originated by Dot Gradations Ltd
Printed and bound in China by South China Printing Company

08 07 06 05 04
10 9 8 7 6 5 4 3 2 1

Library of Congress Cataloging-in-Publication Data
Hughes, Monica.
  Migration / Monica Hughes.
    p. cm. -- (Nature's patterns)
  Includes bibliographical references (p.   ) and index.
  ISBN 1-4034-5879-0 (HC), 1-4034-5885-5 (Pbk.)
  1. Animal migration--Juvenile literature. I. Title. II. Series.
  QL754.H84 2004
  591.56'8--dc22
                              2004000936

Acknowledgments
The author and publishers are grateful to the following for permission to reproduce copyright material:
pp. 4, 7 Science Photo Library; pp. 5, 10, 11, 12, 15, 23 Nature Photo Library; p. 6 Ian West/Oxford Scientific Films; p. 8 Natural Visions/Alamy; pp. 9, 14, 22 Getty Images/Photodisc; p. 13 Paul Hermansen/NHPA; pp. 16, 17 Minden Pictures/FLPA; pp. 18, 19, 20, 28 Natural Visions/Heather Angel; p. 21 Howard Hall/Oxford Scientific Films; pp. 24, 25 Ian Montgomery; pp. 26, 27 NHPA; p. 29 Jean Louise Le Moigne/NHPA

Cover photograph is reproduced with permission of Nature Photo Library.

Our thanks to David Lewin for his assistance in the preparation of this book.

Every effort has been made to contact copyright holders of any material reproduced in this book. Any omissions will be rectified in subsequent printings if notice is given to the publisher.

The paper used to print this book comes from sustainable resources.

Contents

Some words are shown in bold, **like this.**
You can find out what they mean by looking
in the glossary.

Nature's Patterns

Nature is always changing. Many of the changes in nature follow a **pattern.** This means that they happen over and over again.

This kind of bat travels to warmer places for the winter.

Storks spend summer in Europe. They spend winter in South Africa.

Special animal journeys, called **migration,** have patterns. Some patterns have a clear beginning and end. Most migration patterns have a clear beginning and an end.

Migration

Many animals **migrate.** They move from their home to live someplace else. They stay in the new place until it is time to go back home.

Frogs migrate when it is time to **mate** and lay their eggs.

Snow geese migrate in a V-shaped group.

This movement is called migration. There are different migration **patterns.** Some animals migrate every year. Other animals migrate only when they are adults.

Reindeer

Reindeer live in the Arctic Circle.
In the fall, the weather gets colder
there. Deep snow makes it hard for
the reindeer to find food. They have
to leave their home.

Reindeer eat grass,
twigs, and moss. In
fall, the deep snow
covers their food.

The reindeer **migrate** south where it is warmer. They spend the winter in their new home. Then, they return to the Arctic Circle when it is warm there.

There is plenty of grass for the reindeer to eat here.

Wildebeests

Wildebeests live in Africa. In the dry **season** there is very little rain. All the grass has been eaten or has dried up in the hot weather. So, the wildebeests **migrate.**

In the dry season, there will not be enough water in this pool for all the wildebeests to drink.

Huge herds of wildebeests often swim across rivers on their long journey.

The wildebeests move from place to place in search of water and fresh, green grass. When the rains come, they return home. Rain makes the grass there grow well.

11

Lemmings

Lemmings are small, furry animals that live together on mountain **pastures.** Lemmings only **migrate** every few years.

Lemmings do not migrate in winter. In cold weather, they hide in underground burrows.

One lemming may have as many as ten babies each year.

Some years there is plenty of food for the lemmings to eat. When this happens, they **breed** well. Then, there are too many lemmings. So, many of them must migrate to find a new place to live.

13

Green Sea Turtles

Green sea turtles spend most of their lives in the ocean. Every two or three years, they **migrate** to warmer waters near land to **breed.**

Only adult green sea turtles migrate.

14

After the baby turtles **hatch,** they head straight for the sea.

Female green sea turtles dig deep holes on the sandy beach. They lay lots of eggs in the holes. Then, they leave the eggs and go back to where they usually live.

15

Gray Whales

Gray whales spend the summer in the cool Arctic Ocean. They eat a lot of food to build up their **blubber.** When winter comes, they **migrate** south.

Gray whales migrate from north to south.

The whales **breed** and **rear** their **young** in the sea near California and Mexico. When winter is over, the adult whales and their young go back to the Arctic Ocean.

Adult whales can live off their blubber. Young whales get milk from their mothers.

Salmon

Adult salmon live in the ocean, but their **young hatch** in a river or stream. Adult salmon return to the same stream or river where they hatched to lay their own eggs.

Adult salmon can remember the smell of the river where they hatched.

Salmon lay their eggs in the fall.

On their **migration** journey, salmon may swim up rivers and leap up waterfalls. Their young will make the same journey when they are adults.

19

Spiny Lobsters

Spiny lobsters live alone in the sea. Each fall, the sea becomes stormy and rough. Then, the lobsters get together to **migrate** to deeper waters.

Usually, a spiny lobster will attack other lobsters if they come near.

Spiny lobsters migrate in single file, with each lobster holding on to the one in front. When spring comes, they go back to living alone.

Spiny lobsters migrate to warmer water to stay away from storms and rough waves.

Monarch Butterflies

Every year, monarch butterflies make a long journey from their home in Canada and the northern United States. They **migrate** before the cold winter weather comes.

The monarch butterfly lives alone in the summer.

The butterflies rest in the same trees each year when they fly south.

They fly south in large groups to California and Mexico, where it is warm. After winter, they fly back north to **breed.**

Blue-winged Parrots

Most kinds of parrots live all year in a rain forest. Blue-winged parrots are different because they **migrate.** They spend the winter in Australia.

The blue-winged parrot gets its name from the patch of blue on its wing.

Blue-winged parrots live in the Australian rain forest in the winter.

Then, they fly a long distance from Australia to Tasmania. This is where they spend the summer. They **breed** and **rear** their **young** there before flying back to Australia.

Swallows

Swallows **migrate** every year. In spring, they live in the **United Kingdom.** They build nests, lay eggs, and **rear** their **young** there.

Swallows feed bugs to their hungry chicks.

In fall, swallows get ready to migrate. They fly south to spend the winter in South Africa, where it is warm.

Large **flocks** of swallows gather together to fly off.

Arctic Terns

Arctic terns **migrate** farther than any other animal. In summer, they **breed** in their Arctic home, near the North Pole. They stay there until the weather gets colder.

On their journey, Arctic terns feed in the air as they fly.

Arctic terns keep their chicks safe from harm.

In winter, Arctic terns fly very far south to Australia and the Antarctic, near the South Pole. After half a year, they fly back to the Arctic.

29

Migration Map

Around the world, animals make different **migration** journeys at different times of the year. Do you remember any of these animals and their journeys?

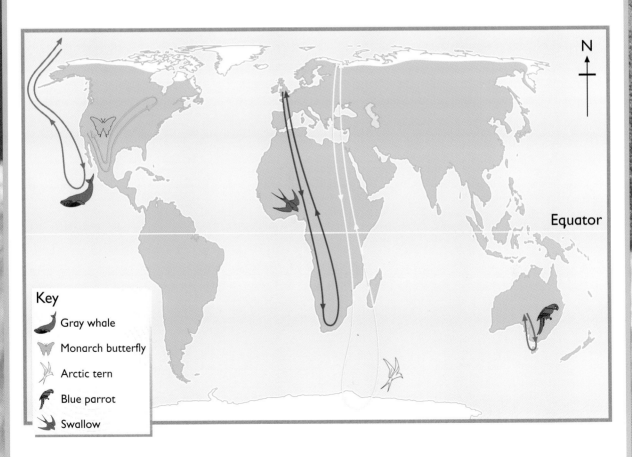

N

Equator

Key

Gray whale

Monarch butterfly

Arctic tern

Blue parrot

Swallow

Glossary

blubber layer of fat under the skin

breed to have babies

female girl

flock group of birds

hatch break out of an egg

mate to come together to make babies

migrate to move to a new place to live

pasture grassy land where animals eat

pattern something that happens over and over again

rear to bring up young

season time of year. Each season has a special type of weather and temperature.

United Kingdom countries of Great Britain and Northern Ireland

young baby form of an animal

More Books to Read

Crossingham, John and Bobbie Kalman. *What Is Migration?* New York: Crabtree, 2001.

Salariya, David. *The Journey of a Swallow.* Danbury, Conn.: Scholastic Library, 2000.

Sayre. *Home at Last: A Song of Migration.* New York: Henry Holt, 1998.

Index